Thailand:

JR's Travel Guide For Millennials

ISBN: 1721740341
ISBN-13: 978-1721740345

Table Of Contents

Introduction: Thailand 101

Planning a trip anywhere is exciting enough. And if the place is tantalizing Thailand, then the excitement is multifold. However, before you go and lap up the fun of Thailand, a little amount of knowledge (in the form of tips, tricks, suggestions, recommendations, etc.) about this kingdom country will help you immensely in being prepared to travel to this splendidly magical land. The preparedness from the knowledge gained will keep you safe, happy, and well-informed, allowing you to make the right choices, and ensuring that your Thailand trip is not only exciting and exhilarating but also fulfilling, rewarding, and unforgettable.

Famous for its marvelous beaches; happy monks; wondrous national parks, replete with fascinating wildlife, including majestic and graceful elephants; to its vibrant nightlife; revered temples and monasteries; an amazing range of delectable foods, and more, Thailand is indeed a paradise on earth. It offers its visitors a variety of experiences ranging from the contemporary decadent delights of shopping malls to ancient legends from its rich history and culture to peaceful boat rides on quiet canals.

In addition to the fabulously famous cities of Bangkok, Chiang Mia, Phuket, and Pattaya, Thailand is home to some beautiful lush-green islands like Koh Phi Phi, Koh Lanta, Koh Samui, Koh Pangan, and Koh Tao (these islands are included in this book). So, let's get straight in and learn more about enchanting Thailand.

Thailand Weather

Thailand has a tropical climate. Most of the areas covering this country have a hot and humid climate during a large part of the year. Northern Thailand is characterized by three seasons while the southern peninsular region has only two seasons. The three seasons in Northern Thailand are clearly defined and include:

- The dry climate between November and May which is, again, broken into two seasons based on temperature (the northwest monsoon effects are not felt much in Northern Thailand)

    o Between November and February, the northern region experiences cool breezes, reducing the temperature slightly

- o During the period between February and May, temperatures are relatively high.

- The climate between May and November is wet, with the effects of the southwest monsoon winds bringing very heavy rains to this region

Southern Thailand experiences only two seasons which are the dry and wet seasons, though they occur at different times for the east and west coasts. The southwest monsoon is a harbinger of heavy rains and thunderstorms to the west coast during the period between April and October. The east coast of peninsular Thailand receives rain mostly between September and December. Generally speaking, Southern Thailand gets far more rainfall than Northern Thailand.

Considering the weather conditions, the best time to travel to Thailand is from November to February during which time the northeast monsoon blows cool air throughout, providing much-needed respite from the tropical heat. The average temperature in Bangkok ranges between 18 and 32 degrees Celsius during this cool period. At the same time, the northeastern and the northern parts of the country experience morning temperatures between 8 and 12 degrees Celsius with the day temperature hovering at around 20 degrees. At nights, these places can get chilly, and in mountainous regions, the temperatures can freeze.

During the rest of the time, Thailand can be quite hot. However, that need not deter a determined traveler if he or she is willing to put up with some weather discomforts to unlock the beauty of this bounteous nation at a slow and luxurious place without the hindrance of other tourists. A word of caution here; even if you are the most determined traveler, it is better to avoid the month of April because it is usually the hottest month right across Thailand.

The period between July and October can get very, very wet with most of Thailand receiving its maximum annual rainfall during this time. In fact, many parts of the country are flooded. The most challenging part of traveling to Thailand during this time is the unpredictability of the weather. There is no constant downpour as in a typical monsoon climate, but you could suddenly be facing the wrath of torrential rains.

Thai Cultural Do's and Don'ts

Displaying cultural etiquette, as per the expectations of the place you visit, reflects the level of culture and dignity you, as an individual and as a representative of your country, have to offer. Showing disrespect and disdain for the people and culture of the nation you are visiting is a forbidden thing in the world-traveling community. Therefore, it is good to be aware of the cultural do's and don'ts of Thailand before you visit the country.

Don't Be Disrespectful of Thai Royalty – Thailand people revere and admire their royalty and all the people and elements associated with Thai royalty. Respecting the Thai royal family is one of the first lessons to learn before you choose to visit this magnificent kingdom. In fact, there is a law (that is taken very seriously by law enforcement agencies and the people) in the country against insulting the royal family.

Do Wear Suitable Attire in Temples – Temples are very sacred places in Thailand and covering up appropriately while visiting a temple is a done thing there. You must wear clothing that covers your head, chest, and knees as much as possible. There are some very touristy places in Thailand where temples allow beachwear in the form of shorts and tank tops. Even here, you must cover your head and chest.

It might make sense to have a scarf or shawl readily available while you are traveling through the country. It would be such an unfortunate thing to stumble upon a beautiful temple and not be able to enter it because of the lack of appropriate clothing.

Do Remove Footwear – Whether you are visiting a temple or someone's home or even some shops, you must remember to remove your footwear before entering. Where shoes are not allowed, you will see a place outside for placing your footwear, or you will see piles of shoes outside the venue.

The people of Thailand believe that feet are the most unhygienic parts of the human body and shoes take an even lower position in this regard. Therefore, any activity related to the feet, including putting them up on the table or touching anyone with your feet, is not just inappropriate but a huge no-no.

Do Treat Buddha Symbols with Respect – Thailand is a Buddhist country, and there are plenty of Buddha statues and sites all over. It is imperative that you treat every image and symbol of Buddha with respect. Climbing statues of Buddha in temples is considered offensive and even punishable by law.

Additionally, there is a law in Thailand that prevents anyone from taking a Buddha statue from the country without a permit. While small-sized figures generally can be taken out without any licenses, anything over five inches in height requires a government permit before you can bring it home. While you might get away with it, it is a punishable offense by law if caught at customs.

Do Respect Monks – The Buddhist monks are very religious people and are highly revered in Thailand. Here are some do's and don'ts:

- Don't ask personal questions

- Bow when you meet a monk

- Don't hand over anything to a monk directly; instead, place it in front of them, and they will pick it up

- If you are a lady, then you must take extra care in this regard as monks are forbidden to have any kind of physical contact with women including brushing past or touching while walking

Don't Touch Anyone's Head – The feet are considered the dirtiest, and the head is regarded as the cleanest and the most sacred part of the human body in Thai culture. Therefore, touching anyone's head even in a friendly gesture is not allowed. You must be extra cautious when dealing with children because ruffling a child's hair is perfectly normal in western culture and is frowned upon in Thailand. So it is important to be conscious of these gestures and avoid touching anyone's head at all.

Do Return the 'Wai' Greeting Warmly – Hands folded in a prayer position with a slight bow is a common form of greeting in Thailand and is referred to as 'wai.' Being an amiable set of people, most Thais will greet you this way. It is appropriate that you return this greeting with the same warmth and friendliness that you receive it. The Thais appreciate this gesture very much.

Don't Indulge in Nudity – Sunbathing in the nude or riding a scooter without a shirt are frowned upon by the locals. Remember that

Thailand is a country steeped in conventional eastern cultures that call for covering up appropriately. Nudity is simply not accepted here.

Activities to Avoid in Thailand

Thailand is a beautiful nation filled with adventurous and wonderful activities for visitors. Unfortunately, this country is picking up a reputation for danger for many wrong reasons driven by the events organized and participated in by the locals and visitors. As a visitor, it is essential to participate in the preservation of Thailand's age-old customs, traditions, and culture.

To do this, you must avoid putting your money into unethical activities, resulting in giving the country an undeserved bad reputation. So it is wise to be a responsible visitor and avoid participating in the following activities in Thailand:

Avoid Ping-Pong Shows and other Sex Industry Related Activities – In addition to the fact that such events are rooted in the exploitation of women, Thailand has become a region of human trafficking activities because of these unethical businesses. There is no way of knowing how the people in these unregulated industries are being treated. Therefore, as a responsible citizen of the world, it is imperative that you not take part in any way whatsoever.

Avoid Standing on Coral Reefs – Coral is very fragile. If you stand upon or even touch coral reefs thoughtlessly, not only will you get hurt but you will be participating in destroying this extremely sensitive ecosystem. A little bit of care and thought can go a long way in preserving nature and her delicate balance.

Avoid Playing with Wildlife – In today's active internet world, one can see many pictures on social media platforms showing tourists holding up starfish and touching turtles. You must realize that these are creatures from the wild which play an important role in the balance of our environment. Avoiding such rashness will help keep wildlife safe and secure.

On the same note, another significant activity to avoid is this; you will see a lot of monkeys and gibbons being exhibited by people as 'pet' animals on the streets of Thailand. Avoid encouraging these people either through donations or taking photos with these poor creatures. In most cases, the unscrupulous 'pet vendors' remove the teeth of these animals using painful and cruel methods.

Even avoid elephant riding for these same reasons. These animals are chained up and are made to wear nappies so that they appear 'clean and hygienic.' They are animals of the wild and domesticating them in the name of trade and commerce is not just unethical but also disrupts the fragile wildlife balance. Please avoid encouraging such activities.

Avoid Fishing in Scuba Protected Areas – Thailand is a notorious hub for overfishing, which is rampant all over Asia. Therefore, it is crucial that as a visitor to this country, you, at the very least, avoid fishing (especially squid-fishing, which is becoming a favorite tourist activity) while scuba diving. The places where scuba diving takes place are usually protected areas where fishing is illegal. Exercise caution and avoid indulging in unlawful activities either knowingly or otherwise (make sure you educate yourself sufficiently).

Avoid Seedy and Sleazy Areas – As a thumb rule, avoid those areas that have a seedy reputation for all kinds of exploitative activities. These avoidable regions represent a misguided reputation of this beautiful and magical kingdom. Many of the entertainment options mentioned above, especially the wildlife part, have an ethical and fun version which you can (and must) take part in during your Thailand vacation.

Thai Festivals and Holidays

Relaxation and celebration are vital to the Thai people. Spending time with family and friends is a crucial element of Thai cultural life. It is good to know the holidays and festivals of this country before your visit there, so that you can be prepared for it. Some of the holidays follow western culture and are on fixed calendar days. However, some festivals are based on the lunar calendar, and the calendar dates for these vary. If a holiday or festival falls on a weekend, then the next working day is treated as a holiday.

New Year and New Year's Eve (December 31 – January 1) are official national holidays in Thailand. New Year's Eve is celebrated with food, music, and dance, and on the first day of the New Year, a large percentage of Thailand's people will visit Buddhist temples to pray for a good upcoming year.

MakhaBucha or Magha Puja – This is a famous Buddhist festival and is a national holiday in Thailand. It is observed on the full moon day of the third lunar month (between February and March). On this important day, ordinary devotees and monks come out together in hordes to listen to Buddhist sermons preaching the tenets of Buddhism.

Chakri Day, April 6 – The present royalty belongs to the Chakri dynasty and every year, April 6 is celebrated as the founding day of the Chakri dynasty. On this day, the entire country stops to pay respects to the ancestors and the present royal members of this dynasty.

Songkran, Thai New Year, April 13- April 15 – These three days are declared national holidays in Thailand and typically, the weekend is included to make it a five-day national holiday. Festivities, parades, and religious ceremonies are held throughout the country.

Water is an important element in Thailand's New Year celebrations. Water serves to 'purify' everything and also acts as a symbol of prayer for a good monsoon which, in turn, will bring a good harvest. People joyously splash water on each other using water guns, hoses, and buckets. Be ready to get wet if you visit Thailand during the Songkran festival.

Labor Day, May 1 – While it is a national holiday, there are no major celebrations on Labor Day in Thailand.

Coronation Day, May 5 – This was the day in 1946 when the present King Bhumibol was crowned king. May 5 is celebrated as Coronation Day every year.

VisakhaBucha Day – This holiday follows the lunar calendar and varies every year. It is celebrated on the full moon day of the sixth lunar month (during May-June). This day is celebrated very grandly to define three important events in Lord Buddha's life: his birth, his Enlightenment, and his Nirvana.

Asalha Puja Day – As per the lunar calendar, this national holiday usually falls somewhere between July and August. It is the day of Lord Buddha's first sermon.

Mother's Day, August 12 – Mother's Day, celebrated on August 12, is unique to Thailand because it is also the Queen Mother's birthday.

Chulalongkorn Day, October 23 – King Chulalongkorn is highly revered in Thailand because of his contribution to modernizing the kingdom country. He established freedom of religion, maintained Thailand's liberty despite the onslaught of European colonialism in Asia, and worked hard to make Thailand a modern, contemporary nation but steeped in old and respected traditions. This day is, therefore, dedicated to King Chulalongkorn and is a national holiday.

Father's Day, December 5 – This is again unique to Thailand as the current king's birthday falls on December 5 which is celebrated as Father's Day.

Constitution Day, December 10 – On December 10, 1932, Thailand became a constitutional monarchy. December 10commemorates the event of the signing of the constitution.

There is also a period of Buddhist Lent between August 3 and October 30. Loy Krathong is another important festival celebrated on the twelfth full moon every year, honoring the river goddess. However, these days are not national holidays.

Chapter 1: Bangkok

As a tourist to Thailand, you are most likely to land in Bangkok although there are international airports in other cities of the country.

From the Airport

There are two international airports in Thailand's capital city—Bangkok, including the Don Muang Airport, and the Suvarnabhumi Airport. Every hour, one shuttle bus leaves each of the two airports, bound for the other airport. These shuttles are free of charge (though you may be asked to show your flight booking or tickets) and run hourly between 5:00 a.m. and midnight.

Transfer between Suvarnabhumi Airport and Bangkok City – Public transport is available in the form of trains and buses. There are trains referred to as Airport City Links that run between Suvarnabhumi Airport and Bangkok City. They run from 6:00 a.m. until midnight every day. There are trains leaving in both directions (from SuvarnabhumiAirport and Phaya Thai Station in Bangkok City) every 12-20 minutes with the entire journey being completed in half an hour. Also, there are commuter trains you can take from Don Muang Airport.

City buses are available from the public transportation center at the airport and you can reach these centers from the arrival terminals via the free airport shuttle services. If you want private vehicles, you can hire taxis or use shared private vans to get to Bangkok City from the airport. Rental cars are also available at the airport. The approximate costs are as follows:

- Airport City Link trains – 15-45 baht, depending on the travel distance

- Public transport buses – 7-21 baht

- Commuter trains – 5-22 baht

- Taxis – 250-400 baht, including toll payments

The above prices are only approximations and may vary depending on many factors including the season of your visit, any peculiarity of a particular day, demand, and more.

Accommodation in Bangkok

Accommodation options in Bangkok range from ultra-luxurious hotels to ones that offer comfortable yet basic living needs. The accommodation you choose is highly dependent on the purpose of your visit. If you are on a business visit, then the high-end hotels in the heart of the city will serve wonderfully.

If you are keen on history and culture, then choosing accommodation close to the riverside will work well because access to the Old City from here is easy. If you are in Bangkok to shop, then hotels close to mega malls are ideal. Whatever your purpose, Bangkok has a mind-boggling number of hotels and other accommodation options.

Some of the top-rated hotels in Bangkok include:

Luxury Hotels

1. ***Chatrium Hotel Riverside Bangkok*** – Luxury five-star accommodation very close to the Asiatique Riverfront.

2. ***Shangri-la Bangkok***–Another favorite five-star hotel with excellent facilities and very close to the Bangkok Riverside.

3. ***The Peninsula Bangkok***– A highly recommended five-star hotel not only because of the amazing hospitality facilities it offers, but also because of its proximity to shopping complexes, night markets, and the Riverfront.

Midrange Hotels

1. ***iSanook Bangkok*** – Located close to the River City Shopping Complex, this hotel offers value-for-money hospitality services that will not disappoint you. Malls and night markets are also close by.

2. ***Red Planet Bangkok Surawong*** – Situated close to Patpong Night Market, this hotel offers all the required facilities for a pleasant and comfortable stay in

Bangkok.

3. ***Navalai River Resort, Bangkok*** – Within walking distance of the Temple of the Emerald Buddha, this hotel is in Phranakorn. Along with fabulous facilities, this hotel is located very close to multiple popular tourist destinations.

Budget Hotels

1. ***Sakul House*** – Located within reasonable walking distances to many popular tourist destinations in the city, Sakul House is one of the most popular budget hotels in the city.

2. ***Inn Stations Hostel*** – Located in Chinatown, Bangkok, it is perfect to stay if you are short on resources and have no problem walking to places. With limited housekeeping facilities, it is just right for young and hip people who only want a place to rest and will spend the rest of their time on the streets of Bangkok

3. ***Lub d Bangkok, Siam Square*** – This budget accommodation is located in Pathumwan and is reasonably close to malls, markets, and nightlife hotspots.

Sightseeing in Bangkok

The Grand Palace – The spectacular, dazzling Grand Palace is an absolute must-see in Bangkok. For 150 years, from 1782 (when it was built), the Grand Palace was the royal court, the home, and the administrative center of the Thai rulers. Its intricate details and excellent architecture are most awe-inspiring. The Grand Palace is the spiritual center of present-day Thailand. It houses many other buildings including the venerated Temple of the Emerald Buddha.

The Temple of the Emerald Buddha – Referred to as Wat PhraKaew, this is considered to be the most important Buddhist temple in the entire country. Housed within the precincts of the Royal Grand Palace, the temple gets its name from the Jade Buddha idol which was carved meticulously carved from a single block of the green stone. The image is placed high on a pedestal and no one except his majesty, the king, is allowed to go near it to perform rituals.

The Temple of Dawn – Called Wat Arun, the silhouette formed by this temple's gorgeous towering spires is one of the most easily recognizable tourist symbols of Thailand. The stupa of this temple is carved with ornate and intricate floral patterns. The Khmer-style temple is nothing short of stunning to behold. Wat Arun is also a symbol of the new Rattanakosin Dynasty and the building of a new capital after the earlier capital Ayutthaya fell.

The DamnoenSaduak Floating Market – This is considered to be the world's first floating market. Today, it has taken on a very touristy perspective and yet offers an authentic floating market experience to visitors who come flocking to this very popular destination in Bangkok.

You can see wooden rowboats laden with fruit, vegetables, and flowers floating down winding waterways, making it a perfect scene for a photo shoot. Food-vending boats that can quickly whip up simple, tasty meals with their ever-ready charcoal grills and cauldrons, such as seafood skewers or noodles, also float here.

Areas to Explore in Bangkok

Chinatown –A pleasingly chaotic and colorful place in Bangkok with a high concentration of gold shops. It is a food haven for thousands of gourmands who flock to Chinatown after sunset to try out the vibrant street-food scene here. The 1km stretch of shopping and food extravaganza is dotted with Chinese temples along with street-side restaurants, market stalls, and of course, numerous gold shops. During major Chinese festivals like the Chinese New Year, Bangkok Chinatown is at its splendid best.

Chao Phraya River and Other Waterways – Bangkok is called the 'Venice of the East' because of its winding and complex waterways, flanked by tall, dense trees and the wooden stilt homes where the locals live. While many of the waterways of yore have been drained of water for fear of the spread of cholera or to make way for modern roads, the Chao Phraya River Khlong (as the waterways are referred to here) is still quite vibrant and relevant.

Chaya Phraya means the River of Kings, and even today, thousands of people use its ferries to get around Bangkok City. Luxury hotels and condominiums intermingle with old temples and churches, and old wooden shacks or stilt homes blend with modern-day street-food stalls on either side of Chaya Phraya waterway. It would be a shame to come away from Bangkok without a glimpse of its wonderful old canals.

Amazing Neighborhoods to Explore in Bangkok

Ari is a contemporary neighborhood replete with a vibrant street-food scene, luxurious restaurants, and coffee shops. Many Westerners who live in Bangkok have made Ari their home.

Thonglor is trendy and is close enough to downtown Bangkok that it makes a convenient place to stay during your visit here. Thonglor is right in the middle of the khlongs, which makes it a convenient place to stay, as you can travel without getting caught in the city traffic. The nightlife in Thonglor is replete with pulsating nightclubs and gaming bars.

Ekkamai is the next stop after Thonglor, if you use the Skytrain to get around in Bangkok. This neighborhood has a good shopping mall and plenty of coffee shops. The most attractive part is that staying here works out inexpensively, compared to other Bangkok neighborhoods.

Shopping in Bangkok

The Bangkok shopping experience is not anything like the typical stroll down a market street or a morning/evening spent in one market. Shopping in Bangkok is a purpose for visiting the city by itself. It is a day-and-night activity and matches the best shopping experience that any western, developed city can offer while giving you the authentic oriental flavor.

Shopping Malls – Bangkok City has numerous shopping malls that will leave you wholly satisfied with your shopping experience. The MBK shopping mall is the place to get some fantastic bargains. If you want to experience trendiness and sheer size, then CentralWorld is the shopping mall for you. Class and glamor are the cornerstones of the Emporium Shopping Mall. And the Siam

Paragon shopping mall takes glamor a few notches higher. Depending on your need and schedule, choose from a vast number of shopping malls in Bangkok.

Chatuchak Market – The Chatuchak Weekend Market in Bangkok is like a market of all markets. Its sprawling size and spectacular variety of wares leave visitors spellbound. Beads, vinyl records, suits of armors, and anything else you can think of, are available in the Chatuchak Weekend Market. Bargaining is happily encouraged. The only point to remember is to be polite and courteous when bargaining.

Floating Markets – The DamnoenSaduak Floating Market, mentioned earlier as a place of interest to visit, is also a great place to have an amazing shopping experience. There are other floating markets all over Bangkok selling fruit, vegetables, juices, local food, and more.

Other floating markets in Bangkok are Bang Ku Wiang Market, Taling Chan Market, Tha Kha, and more.

Things to Do in Bangkok

Rooftop Sunset Cocktail – There are a multitude of rooftop restaurants all over Bangkok which can be a great thing to do one evening after a hectic touring schedule during the day. You can choose from Vertigo and Moon Bar at Banyan Tree or the Sirocco Bar at the State Tower, overlooking the stunning and glittering night skies.

Asiatique the Riverside – This place combines two amazing shopping experiences: the mall and a night market. Situated very close to the SaphanTaksin Skytrain station, there are over 1500 boutiques and more than 40 restaurants, Asiatique the Riverside is perfect for shopping and food. Other than food and shopping, Asiatique the Riverside has a lot of entertainment options like puppet shows, cabaret shows, and more that you can enjoy.

Where to Eat in Bangkok

Bangkok is undoubtedly an ultimate foodie destination. Having to choose from a mind-boggling variety of food places, street food eateries, and restaurants can deter even the wildest foodie. Here are some top choices for you:

Yenly Yours for Mango Desserts – Mango, sticky rice, and ice-cream form a delectable and irresistible combination, and Yenly Yours is a dessert store that is found at multiple locations across the city, including all the shopping malls.

Wang Lang Market – Open every day from 7:00 a.m. to 8:00p.m., the Wang Lang offers a huge variety of food options for visitors and locals. The delicious foods you get here include fried pork, noodles, dumplings, grilled banana, fish cakes, squid skewers, and many kinds of cakes and pastries.

Pad Thai at the Iconic ThipSamai – Pad Thai, Thailand's iconic rice noodle dish, has an interesting history, steeped in nationalistic fervor. The prime minister of Thailand during World War II was Field Marshal P. Pibulsongkram. He led a campaign against the westernization of Thailand and urged people to use and eat Thai products and food.

He started a campaign to eat rice noodles instead of wheat noodles. He released recipes and instructions on how to prepare rice noodles. In support of this campaign, Mrs. SamatBaisamut opened a restaurant in Western Bangkok called Pad Thai Pratu-Phi which got the prime minister's attention and recommendation. All state visitors were brought to Pad Thai Pratu-Phi to partake of the local Thai dish that was slowly but surely gaining in popularity.

Mrs. Baisamutwas, however, forced out of her rented place by her jealous landlord. After this, the feisty lady opened ThipSamai in 1966, and to this day, ThipSamai's history is intrinsically intertwined with pad thai.

Street Foods and Night Markets in Bangkok

Khao San Road - Unlike other cities of the

world where night time is closing time for markets and stalls, in Bangkok, many open only at nights. Come evening, the teeming Khao San Road is filled with visitors and tourists exploring the night markets in search of delectable street foods and everything else that Bangkok is famous for.

Rod Fai Market – Famous as the Train Market, the new Rod Fai Market is very conveniently located in a central place close to the Thailand Cultural Center MRT. Once there, you cannot miss this market's characteristic rainbow-colored tents, selling street foods ranging from typical local Thai fare to nachos to Japanese cuisine and more. The Rod Fai Market is also a shopper's delight.

JJ Green – JJ Green, or Jatuchak Green, is right next to the Weekend Chatuchak Market. Visitors to the Chatuchak Market move to JJ Green after the former closes shop around 8:00p.m. This vintage market combines the features of a flea market and a regular night market. Vintage items are seen on rows of sheets placed on the ground by shop owners. You can see vintage license plates, old car parts, watches, and more. The food options are slightly fewer here than in other night markets, but the vintage items make up for the difference.

Pak Khlong Talat – If you are tired of seeing clothes and foods and other commonly available items in Bangkok, then a trip to Pak Khlong Talat or the Flower Market is sure to brighten up your visit. This wholesome market, open 24/7, teems with gorgeous, colorful flowers that are bound to win your heart.

Clubs and Live Music in Bangkok

You cannot come away from Bangkok without a visit to its vibrant club and live music scene. Here are a few you can choose from:

The Iron Fairies and Co. – With incredible ambiance, coupled with lilting live jazz music, this place is a sure winner when it comes to a live music place in Bangkok. It is located at Vadhana and serves awesome food.

Saxophone Club – Situated in Ratchathewi, Bangkok, the Saxophone Club delivers an almost western pub experience to visitors. Again, there is a live jazz music band playing every day.

Maggie Choo's -Giving visitors a live Shanghai feel, with all things Chinese, Maggie Choo's does not disappoint on the music front. The delectable combination of Chinese noodles, alcohol, and live jazz music is sure to uplift your spirits and enhance the amazing experience of Bangkok.

Spas in Bangkok

The spas in Bangkok are the ultimate experience of relaxation for your body and mind. Helping you unwind by captivating your senses, Bangkok spas are tranquil urban temples.

Spa Botanica – Located right at the chaotic center of Bangkok, the Spa Botanica is situated inside the Sukhothai Hotel. The tranquil spirit of the Spa Botanica is enhanced by a beautifully manicured garden and the sound of gently lapping water. There are some amazing signature treatments, including aromatherapy for both men and women, that will leave you completely and utterly relaxed and unwound.

Banyan Tree Spa – This renowned wellness center in Bangkok is designed to give you the ultimate relaxation experience. With 16 suites and a huge collection of holistic spa treatment options, the Banyan Tree Spa experience, at the hands of trained and qualified people, will leave you very happy and content.

Siam Kempinski Spa – This place offers

customized spa treatments, depending on your body, skin type, and the prevailing season. A visit to the Siam Kempinski Spa, which is directly connected to the Siam Paragon Mall, is the perfect way to relax after a hectic shopping experience at the mall.

How to Get Around in Bangkok

There is no doubt that traffic in Bangkok is notorious and it is very easy to get stuck in traffic jams, jeopardizing your entire trip, if you don't take the trouble of learning how to get around the city. Despite the problems with traffic, getting around in Bangkok is quite simple thanks to its excellent and modernized public transport systems.

The MRT (underground rail system) and the BTS (Skytrain) connect main business areas, shopping areas, and entertainment places. Express boats and river taxis can be used to explore historical sites and other tourist locations. Taxis are reasonably priced, and you will find them in every nook and corner of the city, ready to take you wherever you want to go. Let's look at some of the main transportation options in Bangkok:

Bangkok Skytrain (BTS) – The BTS is a great and efficient way to get around Bangkok.

Nearly all the major shopping malls, the attractions on Sukhumvit Road, the Chatachuk Market, and the Riverside Front are all connected via BTS. BTS is clean, efficient, fast, and very convenient to get around Bangkok.

Bangkok MRT – The underground rail system in Bangkok is very efficient and fast. The MRT rail system in Bangkok stretches for 20km, and its horseshoe-shaped route extends from Hua Lamphong (near Chinatown) in the south to Bang Sue in the north. The frequency of MRT trains ranges between five and seven minutes. The MRT intersects with BRS at

Silom and Sukhumvit stations.

Bangkok by Boat – Traveling by boat in Bangkok is not just cheap but also gives you an authentic feel of the city. There are historic sites and multiple other tourist destinations on either side of the majestic Chao Phraya River, so traveling by boat is a fabulous way to get a glimpse of Bangkok from a historical perspective right up to the present day. A word of caution though; there is an extensive network of boats that can befuddle and confuse the occasional visitor. Make sure you do your research well before attempting to get around Bangkok by boats.

Taxis – Taxiing around Bangkok is also a great way to get around the city. Many of the city's taxis are spacious and new, and they come in a variety of funky colors in addition to the conventional red-blue and green-yellow. However, during rush hours or downpours, waiting for taxis can be quite a bother. Other than these two times, taxis are cheap and are available 24/7.

Itineraries for Bangkok

Depending on how long you are planning to stay in Bangkok, you can vary your itinerary. The following are typical three-day, four-day, and one-week Bangkok itineraries.

The 3-Day Itinerary

Day 1: Historic sites, temples, and the river

Most of the city's historic sites and temples are on the banks of KoRatanakosin, Bangkok's main river. You can easily walk from one location to another once you reach this central place off the Old City. Start off early, after breakfast, because many of these temples and sites close by 3:30 p.m. and there are many places to see.

Grand Palace and the Temple of the Emerald Buddha – Open from 8:30 a.m. to 3:30 p.m. The entry fee is about $13USD, and you need about two to three hours to see the entire site

Wat Pho or the Reclining Buddha – Only a ten-minute walk from the Grand Palace. Feel free to snack on the street foods as you walk to Wat Pho. This reclining Buddha statue has mother-of-pearls inlaid on its feet and is covered entirely in gold leaf. It shows Lord Buddha in the nirvana state. Inside the temple housing the reclining statue of Lord Buddha, there are four other chapels and hundreds of gilded Buddha images seated in the lotus position.

The Wat Pho is open from 8:00a.m. to 5:00p.m., and the price of entry is $3USD. The estimated time needed here is about one to two hours. You can also get a Thai massage done here and if you do, the time needed is more than one to two hours.

Wat Arun or The Temple of Dawn —Open from 8:30 a.m. to 5:30 p.m. Entry is $3USD and the estimated time is around one to two hours.

After the hectic tour of the above historical sites, which should typically take until 4:00p.m., you are bound to be starving. Head straight to ThipSamai, in Banglamphu, for the national dish of Thailand, pad thai.

Chinatown – Located close to the river and perfect for its night market and shopping. Estimated time here is around one to two hours

Khao San Road – The perfect place to wind down your senses after the hectic day. Here you can party with hippies, hipsters, and backpackers.

Day 2: Modern Bangkok with shopping and cinema

If your trip includes a weekend, then the

Chatachuk Weekend Market is a must. Open from 6:00a.m. until 6:00p.m., there is nothing that you will not get here. You can use the BTS or the MRT to reach the Chatachuk Weekend Market.

If your trip does not cover the weekend, then you can choose any of the shopping areas mentioned in this chapter. The Siam area is for the modern shopping experience and you will find plenty of malls. You can eat lunch at any of the malls, all of which have food courts.

Jim Thompson House – Jim Thompson was the founder of Thai Silk Company, in an attempt to revive the neglected art of making silk. His house, located close to Siam Square, has been converted into a museum and it is worthwhile to visit it to learn a little bit of the history of Thailand's silk industry. It is open from 9:00a.m. to 6:00p.m. and the entry fee is 150 baht.

Cinemas in Bangkok – Paragon Mall houses IMAX, 4D, and 3D cinemas and they are among the best in the world. These cinemas show the latest Hollywood movies with Thai subtitles. You can relax after a hectic day of shopping by watching one of your favorite movies on a large-sized couch. A note of caution: a tribute to the king is paid through a video at the beginning of every show and you are expected to stand up for it.

Day 3: Relaxed morning, lunch at the Silom Area, Lumphini Park, and a nightclub or Skybarcocktails

Silom Area, filled with amazing restaurants, is perfect to get some lunch, and Lumphini, Park, a green space nearby, is the ideal place for an afternoon siesta after that sumptuous lunch.

The 4-Day Itinerary

Day 1: Grand Palace, Wat PhraKaew, Wat Pho, a tuk-tuk ride, and shopping and street foods on Khao San Road

Day 2: A cruise on the Chao Phraya River, Wat Arun, and Chinatown

Day 3: Dedicated to shopping, Lumphini Park siestas, Skybar cocktails

Day 4: Trip to the Golden Mount with 300 steps to get a breathtaking 360-degree view of Bangkok, followed by a riverside dinner overlooking the Chao Phraya River

Chapter 2: Chiang Mai

Chiang Mai is undoubtedly Thailand's second most significant city after Bangkok. It is quieter and more relaxed than the chaotic capital city and should definitely be included in your Thailand itinerary.

Getting into Chiang Mai

Although Chiang Mai, nestled in the mountains of Northern Thailand, is about 470 miles away from bustling Bangkok, it is quite easy to get there.

By Air – Multiple daily flights (travel duration of 1.5 hours) run from Bangkok to Chiang Mai by Air Asia, Thai Airways, Nok Air, and others.

By Bus – There are government and private buses between the two cities. Travel by bus takes about 10-11 hours. There are many kinds of coaches, ranging from those with the most basic seats (slightly uncomfortable) to the more luxurious semi-sleeper seats which offer snacks and movies.

By Train – Perfect for train buffs, traveling by train to Chiang Mai might take longer (up to 15 hours) than other modes. However, daytime trains give you the pleasure of viewing some fabulous scenery on the way. Night trains are good too. There are different classes of train tickets, ranging from third class to first class. Prices and specials depend on the type of travel you select.

By Car – You can rent a car and drive yourself to this picturesque city from Bangkok.

Accommodation in Chiang Mai

There are plenty of accommodation options in Chiang Mai, with many hotels spread right across the city. However, a larger concentration is in the Old City and in the area between the Ping River and the moat.

The older four- and five-star hotels are found in Loi-Krah, the night bazaar quarter, and along the river towards Southern Chiang Mai. The newer three- and four-star hotels are lined up in and around the superhighway, which is not at a walking distance from the downtown area.

Luxury Hotels in Chiang Mai

North City Hill Resort– Located in Hang Dong, it is close to multiple tourist attractions.

137 Pillars House – is a charming luxury hotel located along the banks of the picturesque Ping River.

Four Seasons Resort – Nestled in the midst of beautiful mountains, the Four Seasons Resort is one of the best hotels in Chiang Mai.

Midrange Hotels in Chiang Mai

Dusit Princess – Located on Chang Klan Road, Dusit Princess offers excellent value for money and is close to multiple tourist destinations in Chiang Mai.

Montha Hotel – Located in LoiKroh Road and with bars, night markets, and other important tourist spots close by, the Montha Hotel is a great bargain.

KampaengNgam Hotel – Located in Chang Klan, this hotel is also very close to all the important places of interest in Chiang Mai.

Budget Hotels

There are multiple two-star hotels dotting the landscape of Chiang Mai and many of them offering decent hospitality services for the price you pay.

Areas to Explore in Chiang Mai

Wat Phra That DoiSuthep – One of the most important tourist destinations in Chiang Mai, this temple is situated on the mountaintop and houses a revered seated Buddha idol. You can hike up or ride on a bike or use the red communal cabs to get there. A stunning view of Chiang Mai can be seen from the top, provided it is a clear day.

DoiPui – The village of DoiPui houses some authentic Thai hill tribes historical and art exhibits. There is a beautiful garden, replete with a diverse range of local plants and herbs, which you can wander around. Located just a short distance away from DoiSuthep, this visit can be combined with the mountaintop temple.

DoiInthanon – The highest mountain peak in Chiang Mai is surrounded by the national park housing the beautiful wildlife for which Thailand is famous. You can hike or take a leisurely stroll around the park. However, it makes sense to rent a vehicle as you cannot do the entire park on foot.

Wat Chedi Luang – A temple built in 1401 and destroyed by an earthquake in 1545, the Wat Chedi Luang still maintains a beautiful aura about it. The intricately carved massive elephant structures that adorn the temple can still be seen. A temple dedicated to Lak Muang, Chiang Mai's guardian spirit, built in 1940, stands over the ruins of an older wooden building.

Shopping in Chiang Mai

The shopping experience in Chiang Mai is very different from that of Bangkok. Chiang Mai boasts unique and beautiful Thai artifacts and handicrafts. Looking for designer labels in this city will leave you disappointed. There are numerous open-air markets in the quaint town of Chiang Mai and here are some of the popular ones:

Chiang Mai Walking Street – The shopping experience on Chiang Mai's walking street allows you to see and feel the local culture at close quarters. A vibrant spectrum of the town's food, arts and crafts, and music is on display here. This Sunday market is open from 4:00p.m. until midnight every Sunday.

Bor Sang Village – A craft village about nine km east of the Old City. It is famous for paper-umbrella crafts. The beautiful floral patterns are a signature craft of the Bor Sang Village. A little souvenir from here will make an ideal Thailand gift for family and friends back home.

Riverside Boutique Shops – A small section of the Charoenrat Road across the River Ping is perfect for buying local high-end brands of arts and handicrafts. A few old wooden shops in this area have been renovated which now specialize in locally made luxury handicrafts.

Ginger and The House Shop – Located on Moonmuang Road, this little establishment has a fantastic and colorful display of authentic Thailand kitchenware, furniture, and clothing. The funky clothing and bright-colored and intricately-designed cushions are worthy of taking back home.

Things to Do in Chiang Mai

Visit Old City Temples – The Old City is like a museum of temples. In addition to the ones mentioned above, there are many more temples worth a visit in Chiang Mai Old City, including:

- Wat Phra Singh (the second most revered temple after Wat Phra That DoiSuthep)

- Wat Phan Tao (which is very close to the Wat Chedi Luang Temple)

- ThaPae Gate (which formed part of the erstwhile fortress of the city)

The above is not exhaustive in any way, and if you have the time and interest, you will find a lot more temples to see in the Old City.

Chiang Mai Night Safari – With three animal zones including the Jaguar Trail, the Savanna Safari, and the Predator Prowl, Chiang Mai Night Safari offers a range of wildlife activities to entertain visitors. You can hand-feed wild animals (under the strict supervision of qualified trainers), you can pet tiger cubs, and you can feast your eyes on a spectacular laser show. This is open from 11:00a.m. until 11:00p.m.

Wiang Kum Kam – An ancient city that dates back to the eighth-century Haripunchai Kingdom. Located about five km south of Chiang Mai, there are many interesting things to see here including stone tablets with Mon inscriptions, Buddhist sculptures, pottery, and ancient earthenware. Riding on a horse-led carriage enhances the antique feel of experiencing a city of form the eighth century.

Elephant Jungle Sanctuary – Elephants and Thailand are almost synonymous. The Elephant Jungle Sanctuary in Chiang Mai is one of the modern attractions dedicated to the welfare of these gentle creatures. It acts as a retirement home for aged and out-of-work elephants from the tourism and logging industry. The sanctuary provides as natural an environment as possible for these elephants who have given their lives for the benefit (many times, needless benefit) of humankind.

Where to Eat in Chiang Mai

While every street food stall in Chiang Mai serves up some outstanding dishes, there are a few restaurants that are worth trying during your visit to the town.

Food 4 Thought – The ingredients are all organic and locally sourced. There are breakfast, lunch, and dinner options, including vegan and vegetarian options. This restaurant offers authentic Thai food as well as fusion dishes to suit the Westerner's palate.

David's Kitchen - If you want fine dining in Chiang Mai, then David's Kitchen is the place to try. It is perfect to celebrate a momentous occasion like an anniversary or birthday or even to impress a date. The fine dining options here include French and other cuisines. It is one of the most popular restaurants in Chiang Mai and making a reservation is recommended, lest you are left stranded without a table.

Beast Burger – With a straightforward menu on offer, Beast Burger's dishes are cooked very well and you will not be disappointed. With a choice of sauces to go with large, juicy burgers and French fries, Beast Burger should be a place to have at least one meal during your stay in Chiang Mai.

Rustic and Blue – In addition to being a completely organic-sourced restaurant, many of Rustic and Blue's ingredients are grown in their own farms. The brunch items at Rustic and Blue are excellent. They started off as a brunch restaurant but have expanded to include dinner options as well.

Warorot Market – One of the most popular food markets in Chiang Mai. It has an extensive collection of fresh produce and ready-to-eat meals and snacks. The second and third floors of this market house clothing and accessories shops. The quality of items sold here is not exceptional, but the prices are very affordable.

Popular and must-try dishes in the Warorot Market include authentic saioua or the spicy sausage made in the northern style, namprikong, or the dip made with red and green chili, and keap moo or crispy pork skin. It is open from 10:00a.m. to 10:00p.m.

Night Markets in Chiang Mai

Chiang Mai Night Bazaar – Clothing and unique Thai handicrafts and jewelry shops are found throughout the Chiang Mai Night Bazaar which extends from LoiKhro in the south to ThaPhae Road. This market has everything to make your Chiang Mai shopping experience complete. The range of items includes carved elephants, fake football shirts, luggage, DVDs, sunglasses, and plenty, plenty more. It's open every night between 6:00p.m. and 10:30 p.m.

Wualai Walking Street – Very close to the Old City, the Wualai Walking Street is smaller than the other markets in Chiang Mai but offers visitors a leisurely pace of shopping, unlike the Sunday market where you do end up jostling your way through the crowd. The Wualai Walking Street has a lot of locally made products and handicrafts on offer. It's open from 5:00p.m. until 10:30 p.m.

Kalare Night Bazaar – Tucked away from the noise and hustle and bustle of the Chiang Mai Night Bazaar, the Kalare Night Bazaar is a quiet haven to indulge in some fabulous shopping. With an entertainment area and an open food court, you can spend the entire night in the place relaxing with food, drink, and live music after a hectic round of shopping. There are jewelers, clothing stores, accessories stores, shoe stores, tour operators, and many more to serve your every shopping need in Chiang Mai.

Nightlife in Chiang Mai

Chiang Mai offers a wide variety of choices including dancing and drinking to party late into the night. Live music venues are the most popular form of nightlife in Chiang Mai. Riverside drinking is another common and well-liked night pastime for both locals and visitors. People get themselves a chilled drink, sit along the river bank, and have a great time with some good company. Live bands playing rock, classic jazz, and blues tunes entertain riverside revelers.

Nimman Road is becoming a nightlife place for youngsters to hang out with food and live music. Within the Old City walls, numerous reggae bars serve cheap beers with good beats and cushion-laden floors for visitors to laze on. These are great places to spend a night out in Chiang Mai.

Boy Blues Bar – This place has live music belting out blues all nights except Sundays. The Boy Blues Bar has a Jam Night every Monday and is perfect for you to try out your singing capabilities. Located on the second floor, it overlooks the sea of stalls and shops of the Kalare Night Bazaar. It's open from 8:00p.m. to 1:00a.m.

HOBS – The House of Beers has a dozen outlets in Bangkok and has expanded to Chiang Mai as well. Located in a trendy part of the town, HOBS offers a wide variety of beers, live music, and great food too. It's open from 6:00p.m. to midnight.

Warm Up Café – It is the most popular and the longest-running nightclub in Chiang Mai. There is a quieter open-air terrace section and a large room section where the live bands belt out music. Between the live music, the café's DJ plays dance numbers, enticing you to take the dance floor with or without your partner. It is open from 6:00p.m. to 2:00a.m.

Zoe in Yellow – Located near the ThaPae Gate, Zoe in Yellow is a backpacker's favorite. There is no live music, but the place is usually packed with western tourists. There is cheap (and strong) alcohol on offer, and the food is reasonably good too. It's open from 5:00p.m. to 2:00a.m.

Spas in Chiang Mai

Excellent treatment, the best masseurs, and the

most delightful ambiance make spa treatments in Chiang Mai heaven on earth. Here are some of the top-rated spas in Chiang Mai:

Cheeva Spa – A luxurious wellness center, Cheeva Spa offers a wide range of body treatments including wraps and scrubs, steams, massage packages, and more. The treatments in Cheeva Spa combine stress relief and therapeutic aspects to make you feel completely relaxed and rejuvenated.

The Oasis Spa Lanna – Located close to the Wat Phra Singh Temple, the Oasis Spa has courteous and well-trained staff who will leave no stone unturned to ensure you get the best spa treatment here. You can choose from a wide range of international and Asian treatments, all designed to pamper and relax you.

Fah Lanna Spa – The high walls and the bordering plants of the Fah Lanna Spa keep out the noise and stress of the outside world, making you forget that you are right in the middle of the Old City of Chiang Mai.

Other than these luxury spas, there are many other less expensive ones in and around the night bazaars that offer a great spa experience too. Just remember to ask around and choose a reputable one.

How to Get Around in Chiang Mai

Scenic views greet you wherever you go in Chiang Mai and getting around this town is safe and cheap too. While the lack of public transport might frustrate you for a bit (especially after experiencing the fabulous system in Bangkok), you will soon realize that there are plenty of other efficient and cheap means of transport you can use to get around in Chiang Mai.

Songthaew – These are the ubiquitous red trucks or red taxis that are the most common means of local transport in Chiang Mai. Songthaews are pickup trucks converted into taxis with two rows of seats and are the perfect way to meet with locals. You can find these red taxis 24/7 to go any place in Chiang Mai. The only inconvenience is that you must be ready to share your ride with other people as they are picked up and dropped off at various locations along the journey.

Taxis – Air-conditioned metered taxis are available, too, though they are not as ubiquitous as the songthaews. You can find them waiting for passengers at the airport, malls, railway stations, hotels, and malls.

Ride-sharing apps such as Grab and Uber – These ride-sharing apps are not just cheap but very convenient too. Just call for them from the app on your phone.

Bus – The public bus service is not great in Chiang Mai, though there are two convenient shuttle services between the airport and the city.

Tuk-tuks – Inexpensive and noisy, tuk-tuks are found all over Chiang Mai. Tuk-tuks take you wherever you want in the city, and the price is highly dependent on your bargaining skills.

Other modes of local transport include samlor (Thailand's cycle rickshaw), bicycles (you can rent them and cycle your way around the scenic town), motorcycle taxis, and cars you can rent.

Where to After Chiang Mai?

After your visit to Chiang Mai, there are many other places you can visit. Come of the options include:

Chiang Rai – The town of Chiang Rai is about 3.5 hours from Chiang Mai by bus. Its main attractions include the White and Black Temples, with the former being more popular and far more picturesque for photo shoots.

Chiang Dao – Just a two-hour drive from Chiang Mai, Chiang Dao is famous for its hot springs, the Chiang Dao Mountains, and caves. It is the perfect place to visit if you want to go cave-visiting and need something non-touristy.

Pai – About 135 km from Chiang Mai, you can drive down, take a scooter, or even fly to Pai which is very famous for its waterfalls, hot springs, Pai Canyon, and hiking tracks.

Chapter 3: Phuket

Getting to Phuket

Phuket is an island 800km south of Bangkok. It is a separate state of Thailand. Getting here is very easy, and you can use any of the following modes of transportation:

By Air – There are daily flights from both of Bangkok's airports, though most people prefer taking off from Suvarnabhumi Airport. Flights operated by Thai Airways, Air Asia, Nok Air, Bangkok Airways, and others fly between Phuket and Bangkok on a daily basis.

By Bus – You can take daytime buses (to enjoy the scenic beauty) or convenient nighttime buses (where you can get your sleep) to reach Phuket. Bus journeys take about 12 hours, and the prices are reasonable. The services offered in the government-run VIP buses are excellent, and they are a safe option too. The island of Phuket is connected to the mainland via the Sarasin Bridge.

By Ferry – There are ferry services from other islands of Thailand such as Phi Phi and Koh Lanta. If you are traveling from one of these islands, you can take the ferry services to Phuket.

By Train – The closest you can travel to Phuket by train is Surat Thani which is about a three- to four-hour drive from Phuket. There are no direct trains to Phuket.

Accommodation in Phuket

Phuket, being a much sought-after Thailand tourist destination, offers an amazing range of accommodation options for visitors. You will be spoiled with choices for every budget range. Here are some of the popular ones:

Luxury Hotels

COMO Point Yamu – With 79 rooms, the COMO Point Yamu, a five-star luxury hotel in Phuket, is chic, trendy, and stylish. It offers spa services, an outdoor pool, and stunning views of Phang Nga Bay and the Andaman Sea.

Villa Baan Phu Prana – With very few rooms, and overlooking the Bangtao and Surin beaches, this small, exclusive boutique luxury hotel offers panoramic cliff-top views. Phuket Town is 23km away, making this place a hub of peace and luxurious relaxation.

Trisara Phuket Villas and Residences – Located on a secluded hillside, this fantastic luxury hotel has 58 rooms, including villas with private pools, and is only a 15-minute drive from the Phuket Airport.

Midrange Hotels

Silver Resortel– Close to the beach and the food market, Silver Resortel is a popular mid-range hotel with decent hospitality services on offer.

The Frutta Boutique Patong Beach Resort – With clean and hygienic services all around, this mid-range accommodation option is very popular among tourists. Its proximity to night markets and beaches is an added attraction.

Budget hotels are available all around Phuket, and the services and offerings match the price you pay.

Areas to Explore in Phuket

Phuket is the biggest island in Thailand, and there are a lot of places you can explore and visit during your stay here. Here are some of the top-rated areas you have to experience in Phuket:

Kata Noi Beach – A small but beautiful beach with breathtaking scenery, Kata Noi Beach is a short drive from Kata Beach. You can walk on the soft sands or go for a swim in the sea.

The Phuket Big Buddha – Sitting atop the Nakkerd Hills, the Big Buddha is a famous landmark in Phuket. With a panoramic view of the sea, the mountaintop is peaceful and quiet, save for the sounds of the dharma music and little temple bells that keep ringing in your ears. Made from Burmese white marble, the Phuket Big Buddha sparkles wonderfully in the sun.

NaiHarn Beach – Despite thousands of visitors coming to NaiHarn Beach and its soaring popularity, this place has still managed to maintain its original pristine beauty. The crystal-clear water and soft sand makes NaiHarn one of the most popular beach areas in Phuket. With a fabulous range of restaurants set up under large, beautiful trees, you will never be short of amazing food in this place.

Karon Viewpoint – Very close to the Kata Noi Beach towards the south, you have the Karon Viewpoint. It is a popular tourist destination and offers stunning vistas overlooking the beautiful Andaman Sea.

Tiger Kingdom – The Phuket Tiger Kingdom is a place where you can get up and close to Indochinese tigers that are bred and raised in captivity from birth until they die.

Shopping in Phuket

Phuket is undoubtedly a shopper's paradise. Open-air food markets, bustling night markets, shopping malls, local shops, and street stalls all vie for your attention as you walk through the shopping maze of Phuket.

Jungceylon Shopping Mall – With over 200 stores housed in it, the sprawling Jungceylon Shopping Mall has changed the Phuket shopping experience. Branded sunglasses, clothes, perfumes, shoes, electronic goods, and more; there is nothing you will not get in this huge mall. It is open from 11:00a.m. to 10:00p.m. every day.

Central Festival Phuket – This fully air-conditioned mall is just outside Phuket and sells everything from sushi to silk, from laptops to jeans, from barbecues to books, and more. It is possible to spend an entire day in this shopping mall. Open from 10:30 a.m. to 10:00p.m.

Banzaan Market – A contemporary-looking Thai fresh-produce bazaar, the Banzaan Market is just behind the Jungceylong Shopping Mall. Priced reasonably, you can buy nearly all local products from the Banzaan Market without the hustle and bustle of other shopping areas of Phuket. Open every day from 7:00a.m. to 5:00p.m.

Phuket Old Town Handicraft Shops – Consisting of textiles and handicrafts shops, this area is a fascinating and picturesque place to explore and do your shopping. The shops lined Yaowarat and Phang Nga Roads, where several artists and artisans have set up studios. Here the most popular shops include Ban Boran Textiles, Think Positive (a shop for souvenirs and knick-knacks), Ban Boran

Antiques, China Inn, and Siam Indigo.

Things to Do in Phuket

There are many fun and exciting things you can do in Phuket. Some of the most popular tourist activities here include:

A Visit to Phang Nga Bay – The sheer limestone cliffs jutting out of the emerald green waters are a distinctive feature of Phang Nga Bay. There is a wide variety of sheltered fauna on these islands which you can explore on specific tours. A leisurely boat trip cruising around the stunning limestone cliffs is a unique and unforgettable experience.

Similan Islands – Just 30km from Phuket's Khaolak coast, the Similan Islands are the perfect dive site to enjoy the spectacular coral reefs. The crystal-clear underwater visibility enhances the wonderful experience of seeing some of the most colorful coral reefs in the world. The islands are a must-visit place if you are a diving enthusiast. For those not keen on diving, Sailing Boat Rock, on Island #8, is a must-see.

Simply Relax on the Beaches of Phuket – There are numerous pristine beaches all around the island of Phuket on which you can quietly sit back with a drink and some great company and relax thoroughly. There are over 30 beaches in this island province, ranging from highly secluded to crowded and lively. Some of the best beaches in Phuket include Kata Beach, Freedom Beach, Kata Noi Beach, Ya Nui Beach, Surin Beach, Paradise Beach, NaiHarn Beach, Bangtao Beach, and Patong Beach.

Learn to Cook Thai Cuisine – Phuket has a lot of places where visitors are taught to cook authentic Thai cuisine. You can pick up the art of discerning the perfect Thai ingredients and cooking techniques and show off your learned skills back home to family and friends. These cooking classes are available as morning, evening, or entire day packages.

Where to Eat in Phuket

There is absolutely no shortage of eating options in Phuket. There are food places that offer amazing simple staples, and there are elegant fine-dining restaurants that make you feel like royalty. Here are some great foods you must try in Phuket, along with the places that are popular for specific dishes:

Bang Pae Seafood Restaurant for Tom Yam Goong – This is a Thai favorite for nearly everyone who loves their spice. Tom Yang Goong is a mixture of spicy and tangy soup with prawns or pork, noodles, vegetables, coconut milk, red chili, and plenty of herbs and spices. If you do not like spicy food, then this is not for you.

Mee Ton Poe Restaurant for MeeHokkien Noodle – A simple noodle dish, stir-fried with pork, prawns, bean sprouts, and egg, MeeHokkien Noodle is a Thai dish that you will want to try repeatedly. Mee Ton Poe Restaurant is a third-generation family restaurant, and itsMeeHokkien Noodle is a huge hit with both the locals and tourists.

Boon Rad Dim Sum 1 for its Dim Sum – The best kind of dim sum in Phuket is folded over seven times for a beautiful, fluffy effect. The fusion dim sum options in Phuket are mind-boggling. Speak to any of the locals and get advice on the best ones to try before you venture out for Thai dim Sum. Boon Rad Dim Sum 1, one of the most popular restaurants in Phuket, serves this amazing dish for breakfast.

Night Markets in Phuket

Phuket Weekend Market or TaladTairod – Open only on Saturdays and

Sundays, the TaladTairod is a bustling marketplace where you can buy clothes, accessories, custom jewelry, and more. Of course, the foods available are a delectable fare that should not be missed. Open from 4:00p.m. to 9:00p.m. every Saturday and Sunday.

Chillva Market – This trendy and cool night market has a bohemian vibe with a stunning variety of foods, fashion, and other shops. Its distinctive look is created by shops that are made out of shipping containers. Its overwhelmingly local feel is why the Chillva Market is a better night market choice over the others in Phuket.

Phuket Walking Street – Also referred to as Lardyai, which means 'big market' in the dialect of Southern Thailand, Phuket Walking Street is a weekly market, open on Sundays from 4:00p.m. to 10:00p.m. This market consists of Chinese, Indian, and Thai Muslim shops, giving visitors a chance to try out authentic South Thailand cuisine.

Phuket Indy Market – Independent traders have set up shop in this market, instead of professional peddlers. The Indy Market is very popular among young Thais for its amazing homemade snacks and great entertainment scene. It is a smaller and quieter market than the other night markets of Phuket but is definitely worth a visit. It's open on Thursdays and Fridays between 4:00p.m. and 10:00p.m.

Nightlife in Phuket

Bangla Road Nightlife – An after-dark walk on Bangla Road is an experience by itself, and some of the things you see will leave you both pleasantly and unpleasantly shocked and surprised. An open mind is important to have in order to enjoy a night stroll on Bangla Road. It has the largest collection of nocturnal fun things to do including bars, nightclubs, shows, and more.

Night Clubs – The most popular nightclubs in Phuket are Seduction and Illuzion in Patong and Banana on Beach Road. World-famous international and local DJs keep dropping by these nightclubs to give visitors the night of their lives!

Beach Clubs and Sunset Bars – There are numerous beach clubs and sunset bars in and around favorite beaches and mountain areas of Phuket. These bars and clubs combine a fantastic sea-and-sand ambiance; great DJs, capable of thumping out outstanding music; gifted bartenders, dishing out drinks without a break; and talented chefs dishing out great food.

Your nightlife in Phuket is made when you choose to visit one or more of these beach clubs. Some of the popular beach clubs in Phuket include Catch Beach Club, Dream Beach Club, Wassa Homemade Bar, Bars above Kata Noi, and more.

There are also cabaret shows, theme parks replete with myths and legends, live music bars, gay bars, and many other nightlife items you can indulge in, depending on what you need.

Spas in Phuket

There are a multitude of luxury spas housed in five-star hotels, as well as full-service spas and massage parlors dotting Phuket's tourist landscape. Thai masseurs are known to be some of the best in the world, and it would be a shame if you didn't try a spa treatment in Phuket. Here are some trendy choices:

Siladon Spa – A house built with teak and in the Thai style. The Siladon Spa is not part of any luxury hotel or resort. It is a standalone spa resort with luxurious facilities, fit to make you feel like a king or queen. A range of signature spa treatments, including aromatherapy, will leave you spoiled for choices. It is open from 10:00a.m. to midnight.

Santosa Detox and Wellness Center – A full-service spa, vegan and vegetarian meal options, and yoga and fitness classes are all under this one roof. Combining Thai massages and Ayurveda therapies, the spa treatments at Santosa Detox and Wellness Center are bound to rejuvenate and relax you.

Let's Relax Spa – An award-winning franchise and a top-rated full-service spa, Let's Relax offers an excellent choice of treatments ranging from simple shoulder and head massages to full-body scrubs and massages. It is open from 10:30 a.m. to midnight.

How to Get Around in Phuket

There are a wide array of local traveling options to get around in Phuket. Many of the beach resorts are within walking distance of each other. You can also take a taxi or a tuk-tuk to travel around this island province. There are local buses and cars to rent as well. Here are some options:

Tuk-tuks – These are great for short distances but can get very uncomfortable for more than half an hour of travel. Prices are not very reasonable anymore as Phuket is receiving an increasing number of tourists each year. Prices are dependent on your bargaining skills.

Taxis – There are metered taxis, taxis that you have to negotiate the price upfront for, and Grab-app taxis to choose from. They are convenient and reasonably priced.

Songtaews (or local buses) – These are blue-colored buses with seating arrangements and run between 7:00a.m. and 6 p.m. every day. The destinations are also listed in English. Another convenient mode of city transport is motorcycle taxis or rentals.

Where to After Phuket?

There are numerous islands close to Phuket which you can visit after your Phuket trip. Here are some of the islands and places that you will enjoy:

Racha Islands – This consists of two islets called RachaNoi and RachaYai, about 20km south of Phuket. Both these islets are very famous for their snorkeling and diving activities. With a tiny Muslim fishing community living in RachaYai, this is the only place which offers accommodation options. It's rather busy during the day, because of day trippers, but gets relatively quiet after 4:00p.m. You can enjoy a quiet, laidback evening in the few restaurants and bars available here.

Coral Island – Just five km off the southeast coast of Phuket, Coral Island (or Koh Hae) has two absolutely gorgeous beaches including Banana and Long. Coral Island is also ideal for diving and snorkeling. Again, like Racha Islands, it teems with day trippers during the day and is quiet and tranquil after in the evening. With only one hotel, it is the perfect getaway to unwind your mind and body from the hustle and bustle of crowded Phuket.

And if you have had enough of Phuket and its surrounding islands, you can move on to another exotic location in Thailand, Pattaya.

Chapter 4: Pattaya

Pattaya is known for its fabulous beaches which are laid out into three regions including Klang (Middle) Pattaya, Tai (South) Pattaya, and Neua (North) Pattaya. Getting to Pattaya from Bangkok is very easy.

Getting Into Pattaya

Pattaya is just about 150km southeast of Bangkok and it takes no more than an hour and a half from Suvarnabhumi Airport to reach the city by car. You can also travel the following ways:

By Air – U-Tapao, which is 30km south of Pattaya, is the closest airbase. This little airport is an important hub for Thai Air. You can take a minibus from the airport into Pattaya.

By Train – You can take the local train, which starts at 7:00 every morning, from Hua Lumphong Station in Bangkok. The three-hour train ride is cheap and safe.

By Road – This is the most convenient way of traveling to Pattaya from Bangkok. You can take a bus, get a taxi, or rent a car.

Accommodation in Pattaya

Hotels in Pattaya offer more than mere shelter. They combine the famous Thai hospitality and enhance your Pattaya experience with their generous service options. Moreover, as compared to Bangkok and Phuket, the accommodation rates are more reasonable in Pattaya.

Luxury Hotels

Royal Wing Suites and Spa– With a very formidable reputation for excellent service, this hotel has served many celebrities. You can drive straight to this hotel from Bangkok Airport in 90 minutes, and you will find yourself in the lap of luxury.

Hilton Pattaya – Just a few steps away from

the Central Festival Pattaya Beach, Hilton Pattaya lives up to its international reputation of outstanding and luxurious services.

Pattaya Marriott Resort – This five-star luxury resort has a beachfront view and is very close to one of the best malls in Pattaya, Royal Garden Plaza.

Midrange Hotels

At Mind Premier Suites – Located in Central Pattaya, At Mind Premier Suites promises excellent service at reasonable costs. It is within walking distance from many of the tourist hotspots of the city.

KTK Regent Suite – Situated in Central Pattaya, this mid-range hotel is great to stay in and is known for its amazingly good staff that takes care of your every need.

Zing Resort and Spa – Within walking distance from two popular Pattaya beaches, Zing Resort and Spa offers great value for money.

There are budget hotels galore all over the city of Pattaya. Just make sure you do some research and ensure you choose a respectable and reputable place. For budget hotels, seeking local advice is always a good thing.

Areas to Explore in Pattaya

Here are some top-rated places that are worth visiting in Pattaya:

NongNooch Tropical Botanical Garden – Pronounced 'nung nut,' this sprawling park has winding walkways, a topiary garden, a dinosaur valley, and offers a variety of activities for the entire family. If you are traveling with children, then this is a must-visit area to explore in Pattaya. It's open from 8:00a.m. to 5:30 p.m.

Sanctuary of Truth – It is referred to as *the magnificence of heaven recreated on earth* for its massive structure built with wood in the conventional Thai architectural style. The building pays homage to ancient philosophies and religion. Other activities offered here including kickboxing, elephant treks, horseback rides, Thai cultural shows, and more. It's open from 8:00a.m. to 6:00p.m. on all days, including Sunday.

Wat Yansangwararam - Built in 1988 and dedicated to King Bhumibol Adulyadej, this temple is a Thai architectural wonder that is surrounded by sprawling, verdant gardens. Buddhist relics are kept in the main shrine which is on top of a hill. A total of 299 steps lead to this main shrine. The right side of the path to the steps has a lake with a beautiful Chinese pavilion that is filled with artifacts and antiques. It's open from 8:00a.m. to 5:00p.m.

Jomtien Beach – extends for over six kilometers and offers plenty of watersport activities such as parasailing, windsurfing, jet-skiing, kite-surfing, and more. There is also a family fun place called Cartoon Network Amazone that has a lot of water rides and games like spiraling slides, splashing fountains, and other such fun activities.

Shopping in Pattaya

Although not as extensive as what Bangkok offers, the shopping experience in Pattaya can be fun, lively, and enjoyable. Here are a few popular markets in Pattaya that are worth a visit:

Central Festival Pattaya – It is one of the tallest structures on the beachfront in Pattaya. It houses over 300 shops and is the central shopping area in that region. With high-end brands like H&M, Calvin Klein, Marks &Spencers, and more, the Central Festival shopping area offers you a fantastic variety of shopping options. With cinemas, bowling alleys, food courts, and retail shops, you can spend hours together in this place.

Royal Garden Plaza – Stretched along the southern part of the Beach Road, the Royal Garden Plaza is hard to miss because of its signature yellow balloon rising from its structure and the red aircraft at the Second Road entrance. Both these structures are part of the Ripley's Believe it or Not Museum which occupies an entire floor here. The other levels are filled with branded shops. It's open from 10:30 a.m. to 11:00p.m. every day.

Four Regions Floating Market – This is the only floating market in Pattaya. The four regions in the market represent the trade and commerce carried out in the four major areas of Thailand including the north, south, central, and northeast. You can rent a boat and explore this market that is filled with eateries, souvenir shops, fruit stalls, art galleries, and more. Unlike other floating markets found in Thailand, there is an entry fee for this. It's open from 9:00a.m. to 8:00p.m.

Things to Do in Pattaya

A Day Trip to Koh Larn – Koh Larn, or the Coral Islands, are 45 minutes away by ferry or 30 minutes away by a speedboat. They are the perfect day trip to escape the noise and hustle and bustle of Pattaya. Activities on the Coral Islands include underwater sea walking, banana boat rides, parasailing, and plenty of other water sports. Tien and Nual Beaches are worth exploring here.

Art in Paradise – This is a museum of illusion art where you can tickle the belly of a whale, tackle a marlin, and do other fun things with the amazing illusionary artworks on display here. Separate themed zones for classic art, underwater world, dinosaurs, and more are also available here. It is the ideal location for photo shoots. Open from 9:00a.m. to 10:00p.m. every day.

Ramayana Water Park – There are a multitude of themed rides in the Ramayana Water Park which is considered to be the biggest one in Thailand. Serpentine water rides, freefalls, other colorful, gentler rides, a green maze, bubbling geysers, and more make this an exhilarating activity for travelers of all ages. Open from 10:00 a.m. to 6:00p.m.

Mini Siam – Some of the amazing structures and monuments of Thailand and the world are replicated in the Mini Siam park. There are miniature replicas of famous international monuments of Thailand and the world on display here. You can see Bangkok's Wat Arun, Victory Monument, Australia's Sydney Opera House, the USA's Statue of Liberty, and more such monuments standing side by side. Open from 7:00a.m. to 10:00p.m.

Where to Eat in Pattaya

The street foods in all the Pattaya markets will make you go weak at the knees. With hundreds of restaurants and a higher number of independent food stalls, having to choose only a few can break an ardent food lover 's heart. Here are some tips:

Thai Food – These are best tried at the independent food stalls that dot every nook and corner of the city. The best way to choose a hygienic and popular one is to follow the crowd. Any booth that is crowded reflects the quality of the food served there. If you are still not convinced about street food hygiene, many budget restaurants serve authentic local cuisine. The five-star and luxury hotels, of course, give you a fantastic variety of delectable Thai foods to try.

Seafood – Here again, the food stalls on or close to the beaches of Pattaya serve you dishes from the freshest seafood produce available. You can relax on Jomtien Beach with a platter of your favorite seafood offerings and enjoy your meal overlooking the stunning blue waters of the sea. Budget hotels and luxury hotels also serve delicious seafood fare in Pattaya.

In addition to the local cuisine, Pattaya is home to many restaurants and eating places that serve international cuisine. There is no doubt that you will be spoiled for choices when it comes to where and what to eat in Pattaya.

Night Markets in Pattaya

Sukhumvit Road Market – Open from 5:00p.m. until late into the night, this market is right next to Mini Siam. Many of the shops here are open during the day as well. There are a lot more electronic items sold here as compared to other markets in Pattaya. Even if you do not want to shop here, a stroll along this market road is a remarkable and novel experience.

Pattaya Night Market – This offers an amazing value shopping experience. The best night market, it is covered, air-conditioned, and free from the vagaries of the outside weather, leaving you to enjoy your time in the market. You can get clothes, accessories, souvenirs, and a lot more from the Pattaya Night Market.

Thepprasit Road Night Market – This is the most popular market selling local goods in Pattaya. It is located very close to the Sukhumvit Road Market. The most attractive element here is the wide array of street food stalls which are all set up under the metal roofs connected to permanent market stall.

Nightlife in Pattaya

The nightlife in Pattaya is famous all over the world. Pattaya is synonymous with the images of brightly-lit neon signs for discos, bars, clubs, and massage parlors.

Pattaya Walking Street – The Pattaya nightlife experience is incomplete without a stroll down this half-a-kilometer stretch of road. True to its name, motorized vehicles are banned from the Walking Street. Nearly every building on either side of this street is either a club or a bar or go-go bar of some kind. Some of the popular places on Pattaya Walking Street include Lucifer Disco, The Pier Disco Club, Marine Disco, Alcatraz, Baccara, and many, many more. Open from 6:00p.m. to 2:00a.m.

Cabaret Show – The Alcazar Cabaret Show is one of the most sought-after night shows in Pattaya. A team of 400 participants presents a spectacular 70-minute show that is a jaw-dropping wonder. The Alcazar Cabaret Show is a glamorous and glitzy entertainment show at Pattaya Second Road. The dazzling show first opened in 1981 in a 350-seat theater, and today, the theater seats 1200 people and continues to dazzle and amaze the audience. The show hours are 5:00p.m., 6:30 p.m., 8:00p.m., and 9:30 p.m.

Horizon Bar – Housed within the precincts of Hilton Pattaya, the Horizon Bar is right on top of this monumental structure that dominates the Pattaya skyline. The name of the bar is apt because you can almost see the curvature of the earth's horizon in the distance from the high place. It is the perfect place to enjoy a magnificent sunset with amazing food and drinks. It's open from 5:00p.m. to 1:00a.m.

Spas in Pattaya

Thai spa and massage treatments are a matter of heritage as generations after generations have chosen to take the tradition forward. The experienced and qualified masseurs in Thailand (and Pattaya in particular) are trained to offer all kinds of massages, ranging from energizing ones to relaxing and calming ones. Here are some of the best spas in Pattaya:

Rasayana Retreat – Meaning Rejuvenation, Rasayana promises a holistic approach to spa treatments. It offers a wide array of spas and massages that you can choose from, all done under the care of experienced and trained masseur(s). It is located in North Pattaya.

I-Spa Sauna & Spa House – With skin and spa treatments customized to your needs, this full-service spa is located in Central Pattaya. Their range of treatments includes aromatherapy, Swedish massages, Thai traditional massages, body scrubs, and a lot more.

Cliff Spa – Overlooking the Gulf of Thailand, the Cliff Spa is part of the Royal Cliffs Hotel Group, a pioneer of tourism hospitality in Pattaya. With a wide array of scrubs, wraps, massages, and facials to choose from, you are bound to feel completely rejuvenated and refreshed after a spa treatment in the Cliff Spa.

How to Get Around in Pattaya

The Songtaew or the Minibus – This ubiquitous vehicle, found in many places in Thailand, is available in Pattaya too. Dark blue in color, with two rows of seats and a canopy to cover the top, the songtaew in Pattaya is cheap and convenient. You can wave one down when you need to hop in and press the buzzer when you need to hop off. The fare is negotiated before the start of the journey.

Local buses – Although not as omnipresent as minibuses, local buses are available on a few routes covering the main streets of Jomtien, Pattaya, and Naklua. They are convenient but not very regular.

Motorbike Taxis –They are cheaper than the minibuses but less safe too. There are stations to pick up motorbike taxis all over the city, or you can wave down free ones that are cruising the roads. Fares vary depending on the distance. If you are traveling alone, then motorbike taxis are a great way to get around Pattaya.

Taxis – There are no metered taxis in Pattaya. However, there are many taxis which bring people from Bangkok to Pattaya. You are free to flag one of these down and request they ferry you around the city. Taxis cost more than minibuses.

Motorcycle and Car Rentals – If you love biking, then renting a motorcycle is the ideal way of getting around Pattaya. Bikes with automatic and manual gears are available, and you can choose your preference. A driving license is not generally required. However, you must produce your passport to rent a motorcycle. Cars can also be rented to get around. However, the traffic in Pattaya can be quite frustrating, and unless you are an avid driver, it is better to avoid driving yourself.

Bicycles – An eco-friendly, healthy, and efficient way to get around is by riding a bicycle. However, there are fewer bicycle rental places than motorcycle rentals. They are perfect for trips to malls. It is important to bear in mind that the quality of the bicycles may not be very good.

Where to After Pattaya?

The best thing to do after Pattaya is to go island-hopping, especially if you have already finished Phuket and Chiang Mai. While some of the islands of Thailand are discussed in the next chapter, here are a few ones that are very close to Pattaya.

Koh Sak – This U-shaped island was once privately owned and frequented by the rich and famous. There are diving tours to see coral reefs and artificial shipwrecks. There is a place here for history buffs. It is a path going right through the middle of the island in which the footprints of the rich and famous are solidified in concrete. You can see the footprints of Neil Armstrong, who visited Koh Sak immediately after his return from the moon.

Koh Krok – This absolutely gorgeous island is only 100m long. Its eastern shores are sandy, and its western shores are rocky. There is no accommodation available (too small a place to build hotels or even service rooms). However, there are dining options, banana boat rides, jet skis, and snorkeling and diving places.

Chapter 5: Thai Islands

Thailand is home to a multitude of stunning islands, and it is actually unfair to have to choose only a few from them to visit. However, the truth is that it would take many months to visit all of them and not everyone has the luxury of taking very long holidays.

There are hundreds of islets and islands nestled in the midst of the deep blue sea and the beauty of the azure sky above. Moreover, there are many more on the numerous rivers and lakes that dot the countryside. While the large ones, like Phuket, are famous and popular, there are many, many more worth exploring. Here are some of the top-rated ones.

Koh Phi Phi

Koh Phi Phi is considered a superstar island in Thailand as it has been seen in many movies. It consists of six islands, and the best thing about Kho Phi is that it does not disappoint, despite the hype created around it.

Accommodation in Koh PhiPhi

Only one of the six islands, Koh Phi Phi Don, has accommodation facilities. The central area of Koh Phi Phi is between Tonsai Bay (in the south) and LohDalum (in the north). The ferry pier service is located in this central area. There are four sub-areas including Tonsai West (the quietest part), LohDalum, Tonsai Village (both of which are noisier and busier than Tonsai West), and Tonsai East (where most of the buzz is generated).

Tonsai Bay offers a wide variety of accommodation options ranging from dead-cheap budget traveler rates to stylish luxury resorts. Depending on your travel plans and your itinerary, you can choose from a mind-boggling number of accommodation options in Phi Phi Don.

Things to do in Koh Phi Phi

Koh Phi PhiLeh and Maya Bay – Crystal-clear waters, lush tropical vegetation, and white sands are the highlights of the second largest island in Koh Phi Phi. There is only one beach in Koh Phi PhiLeh, called Maya Beach, which became famous after it was featured in a Leonardo Di Caprio movie aptly titled *The Beach*.

Phi Phi Viewpoint – This offers a picture-postcard view of beaches, sand, and the sea. You can walk h the well-trodden path to Phi Phi Viewpoint, located about 186m above sea level.

Where to eat in Koh Phi Phi

Here are some of the most popular restaurants and eating places in Koh Phi Phi:

Grand PP Arcade – Offering American, Thai, and fusion cuisines, Grand PP Arcade opens early enough to give visitors breakfast options as well. It also has a wide variety of vegan and vegetarian choices.

Unni's Restaurant – Perfect for an early dinner before you head out to enjoy the nightlife in Koh Phi Phi, Unni's Restaurant offers a heady combination of fabulous food and stunning sea vistas.

Tonsai Seafood Restaurant – Generous portions, friendly staff, and great views of the beachfront are characteristic features of Tonsai Seafood Restaurant. You must make sure you have at least one meal at this place during your stay in Koh Phi Phi.

Nightlife in Koh Phi Phi

The nightlife is Koh Phi Phi is vibrant and fun without the sleaze that is sometimes, unfortunately, associated with nightlife in Thailand. The many clubs and pubs are in the central area of the island and easily accessible. The music usually stops at 2:00a.m., but the bars are kept open as long as there are customers. Here are some of the best clubs and bars in Koh Phi Phi:

Phi Phi Reggae Bar – Located between LohDalum and Tonsai on the eastern side of the island, Phi Phi Reggae Bar is one of the oldest and long-standing night spots here. Loud music, live telecasts of world sports events, friendly bartenders tending five bars, and a Thai boxing ring right in the middle; all these elements will give you ample reason to enjoy the nightlife in Koh Phi Phi.

Koh Lanta

Located just off the coast of Krabi, Koh Lanta is

one of the most magnificent islands in Thailand. There are over a dozen beaches that are rated as the best in Thailand.

Accommodation in Koh Lanta

This island has the most extensive selection of accommodation options in Krabi province. There are many choices, ranging from high-end to budget traveler.

Andalay Boutique Resort – With beautiful and comfortable rooms overlooking the stunning beach and sea vistas, Andalay Boutique Resort is considered to be the most romantic places to stay. It is a favorite place for destination weddings

Baan Rim Lay Hotel – With very comfortable rooms, and breakfast on the terrace providing a fabulous view of the sea and the beach, the Baan Rim Lay Hotel is another amazing accommodation option.

Of course, there are many, many more options you can choose from to stay during your trip to Koh Lanta.

Things to Do in Koh Lanta

Water and beach activities – Sunbathing and swimming are typical laidback beach activities you can indulge in while in Koh Lanta. All the beaches are amazingly beautiful, with some of them rated as the best in the whole of Thailand. Other than these, you can also participate in snorkeling and diving activities where you can see colorful and gorgeous coral reefs and aquatic species.

Visit the Emerald Cave at Koh Muk – This beautiful location is accessible only by boat, and you have to swim your way through the emerald-green waters under a cave to reach a small but gorgeous lagoon and beach that is surrounded by high cliffs. It is wondrous to behold and definitely worth a visit.

Where to Eat in Koh Lanta

Over the past few years, a lot more eating places and restaurants have opened shop in

Koh Lanta as its popularity is increasing among the traveler community.

Saladan is the primary town in Koh Lanta and has plenty of cafes and restaurants close to each other. Baan Café, which is open from 7:00a.m. to 5:00p.m. Black Pearl, open from noon to 11:00p.m. and Café Mocha, open from 8:00a.m. to 8:00p.m., are some great places where you can get breakfast, lunch, and dinner.

On the east coast, there is the Beautiful Restaurant (open from 9:00a.m. to 10:00p.m.). Fresh Restaurant (open from 8:00a.m. to 10:00p.m.) also offers some great meals.

Nightlife in Koh Lanta

Nightlife in Koh Lanta is more or less low-key. You can meet locals and other tourists in a night bar, watch a Thai boxing match, sing karaoke, or drink the entire night away with your group. There is nothing rollicking about Koh Lanta's nightlife.

Typically, after 7:00p.m., Baan Saladan is full of people who want to shop when the temperature cools down a bit. The eastern part of the island is also fairly quiet during the nights. The highest number of clubs and bars are found on the northwestern coast of Koh

Lanta. There's Cheeky Monkey Bar, which opens at midnight and stays open into the wee hours of the morning. Funky Monkey is another new hotspot that plays a mixture of music including retro, Western, Thai, and more.

Koh Samui

Koh Samui is a melting pot of cultures attracting budget backpackers who come to stay for a couple of months and weekend travelers looking for a short time to relax and unwind. Located in the Gulf of Thailand, Koh Samui is famous for its palm-lined beaches, dense mountainous forests, coconut groves, and luxury resorts.

Accommodation in Koh Samui

Amari Koh Samui – This is a four-star resort located on the east coast of Koh Samui. Its proximity to Chaweng (the central area of Koh Samui) gives it the double advantage of gorgeous beaches and the pleasant hustle and bustle of the central part of town.

Le Meridien Samui Resort – This is a luxury resort situated on Lamai Beach. It offers all the luxury that any established five-star tourist spot provides.

Other than the above, there are multiple other midrange and budget hotels in this island, and you are sure to find something that suits your needs and your wallet.

Things to Do in Koh Samui

Visit Angthong National Marine Park – Made up of 100 small islands and close to Koh Samui, Angthong National Marine Park covers 100 sq km of sea and land and houses a wide array of exotic sea creatures and wildlife.

Big Buddha – Located on the north coast of Koh Samui, the Big Buddha shrine houses golden statue of Lord Buddha. This 12m high statue is, perhaps, the most famous landmark in Koh Samui. Inside the temple, there are other smaller shrines dedicated to Lord Buddha. The streets surrounding the Big Buddha Temple have many souvenir shops too.

Bophut's Fisherman Village – This little village is full of rustic-looking structures and buildings of trendy restaurants, boutique stores, along with a few hotels too.

Where to eat in Koh Samui

The considerable number of restaurants and dining places ensure that you will never have to go hungry while in Koh Samui. Whether you are looking for local fare or international cuisine, there is a place to cater to every taste bud. Chaweng Beach has the largest concentration of food places in Koh Samui. Here are some of the most popular restaurants:

The Boudoir – This restaurant makes you feel like Arabian royalty with its scintillating satins and swirling silks. You can dine sitting on the cushioned divans and soak in the dining opulence it offers.

Chez Francois - It is one of the most popular restaurants in Bophut, housed in an ordinary, nondescript building. The highlight of this place is the famous French chef, Chef François Porté-Garcia, who cooks your meals.

Nightlife in Koh Samui

The nightlife in Koh Samui is rated among the best in Thailand. The full moon parties of this island are legendary and are a major tourist attraction. Visitors are keen on partying on the soft sands of Koh Samui beaches until the wee hours of the morning. While some places serve buckets of cheap liquor, other gourmet places are known for sophistication and finesse.

Delicate Thai dancers, mud-wrestling ladies, and transgender cabarets are all found side by side in Koh Samui. There are nightclubs, sunset bars, beach clubs and many more nightlife places that you can have a great time in.

Koh Phangan

The full-moon parties in this southeast island of Thailand are also quite well-known. The parties on Koh Phangan go into the entire night and are quite boisterous. Most of the festivities take place on Sunrise Beach. However, in addition to these full moon parties, Koh Phangan has a lot more to offer its visitors.

Accommodation in Koh Phangan

In Koh Phangan, you have a wide range of accommodation options. Some of the most popular ones include:

Thanpraphard Resort – Located on the east coast of Koh Phangan, this resort has some outstanding sea vistas and is perfect for adventure and nature lovers. NumTok Beach and ThanPraphard Waterfall are close by.

Viva on the Beach Hotel – Situated on the gorgeous Chaloklum Bay in North Koh Phangan, Viva on the Beach Hotel offers single-room accommodations and self-serve apartments too. It's ideal for both the backpacker and the conventional tourist who wants to stay for more than a night in Koh Phangan.

There are multiple other accommodation options as well. These are only a couple of some of the popular ones.

Things to Do in Koh Phangan

The full-moon parties are, of course, to be enjoyed if your visit coincides with the event. There is much revelry, along with a lot of fun activities during this festival, which you can partake in. Other than the full-moon parties, there are a lot of things to do in Koh Phangan, including:

Visit the Thong Sala Night Market – It is mostly a food market and the seafood dishes are a must-try.

Herbal Sauna Baan Tai – A place founded by the monks and priests of Wat Pho Temple for free use. However, there is a very small token entry fee charged nowadays. Donations are, of course, welcome. Located close to the biggest tree on Koh Phangan, this free sauna is open from 2:00p.m. to 9:00p.m.

Mae Haat Beach – Located on the north of the island, this is a special beach because two types of currents meet here. It is fascinating to see two different colors of water separated by a strip of land. The unpredictable nature of the sea enhances the charm of these differently-colored water spaces on this beach and should be included in your Koh Phangan itinerary.

Where to Eat in Koh Phangan

Every beach in gorgeous Koh Phangan houses colorful restaurants serving delectable meals in different cuisines, including, but not limited to, local Thai, Mexican, Italian, and more. The beautiful and soothing sea breeze will enhance the joy of every meal. Here are some of the popular restaurants on this beautiful island:

Fisherman's Restaurant – Established way back in 1997, this amazing restaurant serves local fare made with the freshest seafood produce. A wide array of cocktails served here increases the joy of eating in Fisherman's Restaurant. Open from 5:00p.m. to 10:00p.m.

Jumpahom Restaurant – Serves authentic Thai fares at low prices. With a simple and rustic ambiance, Jumpahom Restaurant is open from 9:00a.m. to 10:00p.m.

Nightlife in Koh Phangan

Nightclubs, reggae bars, and live music places can be found in almost all of the beaches of Koh Phangan.

Reggae Bars in Chaloklum – There are numerous reggae bars in Chaloklum, nearly all of which offer great food, good music, and a fabulous night ambiance.

The Full Moon Party – Koh Phangan Full Moon Party's primary home is on Haad Rin Beach, the southernmost tip of this fabulous island in a crescent cove. Over 12 powerful sound systems convert the 800m beach into the most famous open-air club in the world. Of course, this extravaganza happens only on full moon nights. This event is on the bucket list for many world travelers and, if possible, you must try and time your Koh Phangan visit around this monthly party.

Koh Tao

Koh Tao translates to 'Turtle Land' in the local language. And true to its name, it is a hub for scuba diving activities. White-sand beaches, the crystal-clear blue waters of the Gulf of Thailand, and vibrant reefs are the characteristic features of the wonderfully amazing island. Koh Tao is 55km north of Koh Samui.

Accommodation in Koh Tao

Some of the most popular hotels in Koh Tao are:

***The Place* -** There are luxury boutique villas replete with infinity pools that are housed in this most romantic hotel in the world (as rated by TripAdvisor). Nestled in the hills that hover above Sairee Beach, The Place offers stunning views of crystal-clear waters and palm-lined shores.

Koh Tao Royal Resort – A beachfront three-star hotel, located within walking distance from the various hotspots of Koh Tao. It offers great services at reasonable prices which is the primary reason for its popularity among tourists to Koh Tao.

Other than the two mentioned above, there are a wide array of accommodation options in this beautiful island to suit every traveler's needs and budget.

Things to Do in Koh Tao

Haad Tien – Also known as the 'Rocky Beach,' Haad Tien has the clearest and the cleanest waters you can lay your eyes on. While snorkeling here, you can see a huge number of reef sharks and, therefore, it is also referred to as 'Shark Bay.'

John-Suwan Viewpoint – This is the southernmost tip of Koh Tao. From here, you will be spellbound by the sight of the northern silhouette of the island. From John-Suwan

Viewpoint, you can see Haad Tien beaches, Chalok Baan Khao Bay, and the hilly, verdant interiors of the island. The place is named after two friends who discovered it while searching for a site to build a home.

Koh Nangyuan – A small group of three islets lying just off Koh Tao's northwestern coast. The beach that connects the three islands is spectacularly beautiful and, therefore, is a preferred photo shoot location for many travelers. Despite the crowds during the day (you cannot stay the night), it is worthy of a visit.

Where to Eat in Koh Tao

There is no shortage of dining places serving delicious Thai cuisine, especially seafood, in Koh Tao. There are plenty of restaurants where you can eat what you want, ranging from simple rice dishes to exotic international cuisines including Aussie grills, Indian curries, French and Italian fine dining, and more. Most of the eating places are found on Sairee Beach and Mae Haat Beach.

Nightlife in Koh Tao

Sairee Beach, in Koh Tao, has a notorious reputation for its nightlife. Starting from beach bars in the north, most revelers work their way to the southern part, hopping from nightclub to nightclub. Fire shows, house music, great food, and plenty of liquor are the highlights of these night parties on Koh Tao beaches.

Some of the most noted nightlife places on Sairee Beach include The Castle, FIZZ Beach Lounge, the Vibe, and the Lotus. The other beaches of Koh Tao do not have the same reputation in terms of nightlife activities.

Chapter 6: Miscellaneous Information

Itineraries

Thailand 3-4-day itinerary

With only three or four days in Thailand, the only place you can cover is Bangkok with, perhaps, a single-day trip to Pattaya.

Thailand 6-day Itinerary

- Days 1 and 2 – Bangkok

- Day 3 – Pattaya

- Day 4 – Phuket

- Days 5-6 –Chiang Mai and Chiang Rai

Thailand 10-day Itinerary

This will be the ideal length for your Thailand trip. Here is a sample itinerary

- Day 1 – Relax and get rid of jet lag in your hotel in Bangkok

- Days 2-4 – Bangkok

- Days 5-6 – Phuket and Pattaya

- Days 7-8 – Chiang Mai and other islands close by

- Days 9-10 – Choose two or three islands that you want and explore them to finish off your Thailand trip

Thai Food Guide

Here are some of the most renowned and absolutely delicious Thai dishes that you must try while in Thailand, irrespective of the duration of your stay.

Tom Yum Goong – This spicy, tangy soup is not just delightful but is considered to be the ultimate representation of Thai flavor. Made with shrimp, tomatoes, galangal, lemongrass, mushrooms, chilis, onions, and kaffir lime leaves, be prepared to be hit by spice and tang that you will never forget for a long time to come. Be warned that if you are allergic to spice, then you should avoid it.

Soup Neua – Soup Neua, or beef soup, is a delicacy in South Thailand which has a higher percentage of Muslim population than the northern part of Thailand (where beef is not very prevalent). Soup Neua is beef broth that is boiled until the meat is tender and then combined with lime leaves, onions, and chilis. It is the ultimate comfort food for any beef lover.

Tom Jap Chai – This is a Chinese soup made with cabbage and greens (typically, mustard greens) which are boiled for hours until they completely disintegrate into the soup. Pork or chicken is added for the meaty flavor. It is not spicy at all but is deliciously flavorsome.

Coconut Milk Curry with Rice Noodles – The coconut curry is made with fish and vegetables and served over rice noodles. The coconut milk and lime flavor give it the unmistakable Thai connection.

Thai Green Curry Chicken – The rich, coconut milk-based green curry is synonymous with Thailand and when you pair this spice mixture with chunks of chicken, what you get is a heaven-on-earth feeling in your palate. Eating this with steamed rice will make it one of the most delicious dishes in the world.

Pad Thai – Already discussed in one of the earlier chapters in this book, pad thai is considered to be the national dish of Thailand. Made with rice noodles, eggs, meat of your choice, lime juice, and other spices, it is a complete meal by itself and a must-try while in Thailand.

Pad Kra Pao – This is minced chicken or pork stir-fried with chilis and basil and served over rice. This simple (and not spicy, at least as per Thai standards) is to die for. Try it from any of the reputable food stalls in any of Thailand's night markets.

Mango Sticky Rice – This amazingly delicious dish combines sticky rice, mangoes, and coconut cream syrup. You cannot really go wrong with that deadly combination, can you? The mango sticky lives up to the sweet and sticky expectations of its name. Don't leave Thailand without trying it (at least once a day).

Safety in Thailand

Like any country that thrives on tourism, there

are good and bad aspects in Thailand. The safety aspect is more or less average when talking about Thailand as an entire country. Some places are very safe, and some places pose a safety risk. Being aware of safety risk elements and being prepared for them will enhance the joy and fun of your trip. Here are some tips that will help you stay safe:

Always remain visible – Avoid going to remote places alone. Stay visible to other people at all times. Walking alone on an uninhabited beach does sound like fun. But if you don't have someone to call for and who can come quickly to your aid during emergencies, then avoid those places.

Don't Flash Your Money Around – Don't take out wads of currency in public places. Be discreet while making payments and pull out one or two notes at a time. In fact, keep money in different pockets and in small amounts so that you can use it as the need arises.

Never let go of your passport – Some rental places might ask you to keep your passport as a lien for the vehicle you are renting. Don't do business with such agencies. Many people have lost their passports this way. Just find another rental place.

Connect with other travelers and stick together – There is safety in numbers, and it makes sense to identify and mingle with other travelers and form a big group and travel together. It is quite possible to do this because most travelers head for the same place at the same time. Of course, it is also important to exercise caution with regard to whom you befriend and not to trust anyone blindly.

Behave responsibly and like an adult – You must remember that you are in a foreign country and away from your family. If you get excessively drunk, you really cannot call your parents or your best friend to come and pick you up. Behave responsibly and ensure you don't get unduly carried away by the full-moon parties and some of the suspicious activities involved in them. Avoid such places if you know you are not going to like it. There is a lot more in Thailand than the small fraction of reported sleaze and entirely avoidable activities.

Keep different payment options handy – Don't depend only on credit cards or only on cash. Make sure you have a combination of different payment options available so that you don't get stuck even if you lose something.

Keep backups of all your documents – Keep hard copies of your passport and other documents. Carry a soft copy, if you can. Or mail the soft copies to yourself or save them on cloud storage so that you can retrieve them from any place that is internet-enabled.

What to Pack for Thailand

Here are some tips you can use to ensure you pack the right things for your trip to Thailand:

Slip-ons – You will be slipping your shoes or slippers on and off at most of the locations in Thailand, be it before entering a temple or going for a swim on the beaches. Having slip-ons handy will ensure you don't waste time and effort putting on and removing your laced shoes. Moreover, the comfort of slip-ons is great for walking, which you will be doing a lot of in Thailand.

Hiking Shoes – In the mountainous regions of Thailand, there will be plenty of hiking opportunities. Carry sturdy shoes for such hikes. The stunning views at the end of a climb will not disappoint at all. You don't want to be left behind for lack of proper hiking footwear. Remember that you will not need hiking boots; just sturdy and simple sandals or shoes good for climbing and walking comfortably.

Water Bottle – There are many places in Thailand where you can refill a bottle with clean, filtered water for a few cents or pennies. Carry a bottle around so that you always have access to clean drinking water—and you will need lots of it in the hot and humid Thailand climate.

Sunscreen and Bug Spray – Carry a bottle of each in your luggage. You can buy them when you land in the country but they may not be the same ones you are used to. So it is wise to carry sunscreen and bug spray from your home country.

Rain Jacket – The rains in Thailand are highly unpredictable, and even in non-rainy seasons, you can encounter torrential downpours. Between hikes, taxi or bike rides, or anywhere else, a rain jacket will keep you from getting wet from the beautiful yet capricious Thailand rains. For the same reason, it makes sense to carry a dry sack or rain fly for your hand baggage that you will be carrying during your day trips. Your belongings will remain dry and safe.

Sweatshirt or sweater –Thailand's climate will not warrant a sweater or a sweatshirt. However, many of the buses and planes have chilly air-conditioning that could freeze you. For such occasions, keep one sweater or sweatshirt in your baggage.

Swimwear and sarongs – Swimming holes, lagoons, lakes, and beaches are all over Thailand, and if you don't have appropriate clothing, then it will be a shame. Carry appropriate swimwear and a quick-dry towel. Sarongs are great for women to wrap around themselves when not in the water.

A Strong Daypack – Make sure your daypack is strong and sturdy and one that goes across your shoulders. The strength will ensure you can put a lot of items into it and also prevent it from being snatched easily by bag-snatchers.

Clothes for warm weather – The weather in Thailand, as already explained in the first chapter, is mostly hot. So make sure your outfits are suitable for warm weather only. Moreover, it is important to remember that the Thais do frown upon very revealing clothes and it is better to be conservative in this regard. Strappy tops for ladies, very short shorts for men and women, and going shirtless are all a no-no. Be prepared for some amount of conservativeness in your dress sense.

Converter – While most of the charging points in Thailand are similar to the ones available in Canada and the US, some hotels have Type C outlets. Carrying a universal charging converter will be very useful. Having devices that run out of battery can be quite frustrating.

How to Get to Other Destinations in Thailand

Flying Around in Thailand - Bangkok is one of the most important cities and trade hubs in Southeast Asia with over 70 different airlines operating here. In addition to the international Airport Suvarnabhumi in Bangkok, there are international airports in many other cities including Phuket, Chiang Mai, Koh Samui, and Hat Yai. There are domestic airports in many other cities and towns as well. Flying to other destinations in Thailand is quite easy, convenient, and reasonably priced, too, thanks to the multiple budget operators setting up shop in the country.

Getting Around Thailand by Train – While low-cost flights within Thailand can be very convenient for most overseas travelers, train buffs can get the pleasure of seeing other destinations in Thailand by train. There are

2500 miles of railway lines in the country, connecting many important destinations such as Bangkok, Chiang Mai, Surat Thani, etc. Some of the railway lines connect to neighboring countries such as Malaysia, Lao, and Cambodia. Train travel takes longer than bus travel.

Getting Around Thailand by Bus – Buses crisscross right across the entire country, and there are very few places that you cannot travel to by bus in Thailand. There are local, express, first class, second Class, VIP, and super VIP bus types, in increasing order of comfort, amenities offered, speed of travel, and cost. You can travel by road by hiring taxis or cars too.

Getting Around Thailand by Ferry – Ferries are a popular mode of local travel within Thailand. However, most of the ferries are full (to the point of travelers being cramped together like sardines in a tin), and not very safe. There are ferry accidents (capsizing because of overcrowding) happening everywhere in the country. Despite the risky elements, it is a mode of travel available to you. And there are some places which you can get to only by ferry.

How to Go to Other Countries from Thailand

Thailand shares land borders with many southeast countries such as Malaysia, Laos, and Cambodia. It is convenient and affordable to go to these and other neighboring states from Thailand, giving you the flexibility to include them in your Southeast Asia travel itinerary.

Moreover, since Bangkok is one of the most important air hubs in the region, numerous flights operate in and out of neighboring and other Asian countries. Of course, each nation has its own set of visa regulations, depending on its diplomatic arrangement with your home country, and you will have to abide by those regulations.

Burma is another neighboring country which shares land borders with Thailand. However, there is very restricted travel access between the two nations and Westerners can travel to Burma (now called Myanmar) only for a day-trip. Cambodia, on the other hand, allows for western travelers to come in from Thailand through various checkpoints. Laos and Vietnam can also be reached via road from Thailand.

Tourist Visas for Thailand

A tourist visa to Thailand allows travelers to stay for 15-30 days (if you come in by land), depending on your itinerary. If you fly in, tourist visas are typically issued for 30- to 60-day periods. Tourist visas are stamped on arrival to Bangkok or Thai embassies located in your home country.

There are a few countries whose citizens are exempt from having to get a tourist visa. These countries include Australia, Brazil, France, Germany, Italy, Japan, the UK, the USA, and many more. Many European and Western nations are covered by this tourist exemption. However, it must be noted that the visa exemption is strictly for tourist visas and not for other kinds of work permits.

The following documents are needed to obtain a Thailand tourist visa:

- Passport or other travel document

- Duly completed visa application form

- Passport-size photos

- Round-trip ticket

- Proof of your financial status

Directory

Tourism in Thailand is a vibrant and dynamic industry. The government is dedicated to offering a great experience for every kind of tourist. With that in mind, the tourism department has a highly relevant and regularly updated website with emergency contact numbers and other important details displayed.

- Directory assistance – 1133 (in Bangkok), 183 (upcountry)

- AT&T direct service – 001-999-1111-1

- Mobile police – 191

- Fire brigade – 199

- Tourist police – 1155

- Tourist service center – 1672

- Highway police – 1193, 0-2354-6007

Suvarnabhumi Directory

- Airport number – +66-2-2132-1888

- Call center number – 1722

- Lost property counter – +66-2132-1880

- Left baggage service– +66 2134-7795

- Tourist police – +66 2132-1155

- Security control center – +66 2132-4000

- Taxi service counter – +66 2132-0360

- AOT limousine service – +66 2134-2323

- Tourist service center – +66 2134-0040

State Railway of Thailand – 1690

Air-conditioned Bus Stations

- East – 0-2391-8097, 0-2391-2504

- North and northeast – 0-2396-2852 to 66

- South – 0-2894-6122

- Immigration division – 0-2141-9889

- Port authority of Thailand – 0-2269-3000

- BTS hotline – 0-2617-6000

- MRT – 0-2354-2000

Tourism Authority of Thailand

- Head office – 0-2250-5500

- Chiang Mai – 0-5324-8604, 0-5330-2500, 0-5324-8607

- Krabi – 0-7562-2163, 0-7561-2811 to 2

- Pattaya – 0-3842-8750, 0-3842-7667, 0-3842-3990

- Phuket – 0-7621-1036, 0-7621-2213

- Samui – 0-7742-0504, 0-7742-0722

Made in the USA
Lexington, KY
28 November 2018